HANDPICKED

HANDPICKED

Simple, Sustainable, and Seasonal Flower Arrangements

Ingrid Carozzi
of TIN CAN STUDIOS

Text EVA NYQVIST • Photographs PAUL BRISSMAN

Abrams, New York

For Stella

Editor: Laura Dozier
Designer: Najeebah Al-Ghadban
Production Manager: Denise LaCongo

Library of Congress Control Number: 2016941969

ISBN: 978-1-4197-2389-6

Printed and bound in China
10 9 8 7 6 5 4 3 2 1

Abrams books are available at special discounts when purchased in quantity for premiums and promotions as well as fundraising or educational use. Special editions can also be created to specification. For details, contact specialsales@abramsbooks.com or the address below.

ABRAMS
The Art of Books

115 West 18th Street
New York, NY 10011
www.abramsbooks.com

CONTENTS

—

Introduction

I have yet to meet a person who doesn't like flowers. Everyone loves to be surprised by a bouquet, and who hasn't picked up some flowers on the way home from work? Nothing transforms your home like freshly cut flowers; they bring a sense of joy and beauty as only children and music can.

Books can also transform the home, giving a room new life and purpose. I love books and I was overjoyed when I was asked to bring this book from Sweden, where it was first published, to the United States, where I have made my home for the past fifteen years.

The world of floral design is in the midst of a transformation, and much of this can be traced back to Brooklyn, where I live and work. Here we tend to focus more on the natural and loose styles that I've come to love, with less emphasis on traditional rules, leaving room for us to create something innovative and exciting. So I am thrilled at the opportunity to share these new ideas on flower arrangements in *Handpicked*—including how I recycle and reuse objects not traditionally used for displaying flowers. I hope this book will inspire you, and that you find my ideas and guidance useful—that, over the years, this book will get stained and dog-eared, like my cookbooks, and that you will make notes in the margins.

I have only been a florist for a few years. It was a confluence of luck, timing, and my background that led me to this field. I was born in Canada to a Swedish mother and an Italian father and spent most of my childhood moving around. My parents weren't artists, but they certainly appreciated art, and both had an eye for design. Sometimes we would have a garden, sometimes a porch or a terrace, but wherever we set down our temporary roots, my mother made sure there were potted plants and flowers. My father was an avid amateur photographer, capturing our lives with his Hasselblad camera. I love taking pictures, too, most often of my beautiful daughter, Stella, and my flowers. Photographs document moments that would otherwise fade away, creating memories for us to cherish forever. I was so pleased to see that Paul, the photographer for this book, works with the same type of camera as my dad!

Before getting my art degree from Parsons School of Design, I worked as an event planner for the Swedish-American Chamber of Commerce in New York. When my former boss called me up in 2012, it had been a few years since I'd left, so I was surprised when she asked if I would work on an event for them. It was a symposium called From Farm to Fork, a black-tie affair where growers, chefs, and food purveyors are invited to share their philosophies and ideas on food and sustainability over a great meal. She wanted me to come up with a design concept for the event, focusing on flower arrangements.

I love a challenge, and sometimes you just have to trust the people who put their trust in you. I had no previous experience with flowers, but as a designer, I knew concept development. My thoughts went immediately to what brought all these people together: fresh produce and sustainability!

The result was flower boxes built from salvaged wood and filled with artichokes, crown dill, decorative cabbages, berries, and natural-looking flowers, which I show several examples of in this book (SEE PAGES 113 AND 127). The From Farm to Fork event was a huge hit, and has become a yearly event for the Chamber. And it certainly was a big deal for me, too.

The event industry can be unnecessarily wasteful. During my time as an event planner, I witnessed over and over how a whole party venue was cleared out. Everything, from untouched food platters to beautiful flower arrangements in their vases, was stuffed into garbage bags and tossed into a dumpster. I figured there had to be a better way.

At the end of that first event, I collected all my flowers and brought them with me back to Brooklyn. The next day I stuck a few arrangements in my bicycle basket and started to deliver them to local business owners in my area. They were so happy to receive these gifts, and the next time they or someone they knew needed flowers for an event, they called me, because they had seen my work. I never had to advertise or do any traditional marketing—my flowers spoke for me! And that is how my business started: door to door, gift by gift.

The people I know on this side of the Brooklyn Bridge are especially keen on recycling things, reclaiming old building materials, and repurposing stuff that otherwise would have ended up at the dump. This has raised awareness of sustainability as a worthy cause, for sure, but it has also laid groundwork for the ever-evolving cool and eclectic style that is the essence of the Brooklyn brand. When the Brooklyn Flea opened in Williamsburg in 2008, it was evident just how great the yearning for everything old, or secondhand, had become. More and more people were looking for items with soul and character. At that time, I was working as a designer for Recycled Brooklyn, a company that builds furniture from salvaged wood and metal. I had a small space there that I really liked, but as my business took off, and theirs grew, too, it was time to move on. And that is how I came to set up shop in the space that is now called Tin Can Studios.

When I started to build my business, I hesitated at first to take on weddings. They seemed unnecessarily stressful. But I'm so glad I decided to go in this direction, since in addition to branded and corporate events, weddings are now one of our main focuses. Not much is more satisfying than being able to contribute to the beauty of a wedding, to share such a happy day. In Brooklyn, we also have some of the most amazing wedding venues, from wineries and rooftops to tiny backyards, old stables, and raw spaces, such as the Wythe Hotel and Pioneer Works (SEE PAGE 22). This environment has informed my aesthetic and the overall approach to flower arranging that you'll see in the pages to follow.

I am lucky to live and work in an area close to some of the best and most reliable flower growers on the East Coast, and, whenever possible, I source locally and seasonally. Choosing local is, of course, better for the environment, but also provides me with the best flowers. I can easily see if flowers were locally grown or if they spent days in transit. Moreover, many of my favorite blooms, such as dahlias and ranunculus, grow here in New York, though sometimes, when working with big events in the dead of winter, or when a client makes special requests, I do have to rely more on imported flowers. However, I do

whatever I can to act responsibly, including reducing waste on my end. After my events I bring back everything I can for repurposing. I also forage for weeds whenever possible. It's amazing what plants sprout and grow in asphalt cracks and along city highways. I also hope to be able to grow my own flowers on my rooftop someday!

Every flower in this book is hand-selected, or "handpicked," and so is every vase, bowl, and crate. Whenever I go to the flower market, I visit all of the different vendors and carefully look through the buckets of blooms for whatever is in season and looks the freshest, strongest, and prettiest. Then I select what will work with my color palette and style that day. There is always one selection that is better suited for the arrangements I am making (and that's the one I want). The same goes for vases—though several might work, one of them works the best with the flowers I have picked. Throughout this book, I offer a look into my selection process and an overview of the elements that I consider essential.

Here I present a variety of options for the at-home florist. Since I am a professional, I have the luxury to pick and choose—within a given budget, of course—among the best flowers available on the market. For each arrangement, I often include ten to fifteen different varieties. I wish everybody could do the same, but I know that's not the case; therefore, among these pages you'll find plenty of arrangements you can make with flowers from a supermarket or corner deli, using just a few different types. (It's also important to note that the techniques and step-by-step instructions I show here can be applied to almost any flower combination—even weeds!) Some of my professional work is also included for inspiration, as well as a few more elaborate arrangements you might want to try for a special occasion.

In the pages to follow, I share some of the knowledge and tricks I've learned along the way, but please, please don't be afraid to do your own thing. There is no right or wrong here. I really believe in the fun and spontaneity of arranging flowers, in choosing what's available, and in using what's at hand. That is my philosophy and that is how I built my business. Flowers from the supermarket or corner bodega can be as pretty as the ones from expensive flower shops, and if I can find plants to pick in Brooklyn, I am sure you can find them wherever you are, too! In the back of this book (SEE PAGE 155), I list some sources where you can find flowers, tools, and nontraditional vases. Also there is a list of comparable replacements for my favorite blooms, so that you can easily make adjustments based on preference or availability (SEE PAGE 152).

I am inspired by everything and everyone, and the idea that every day brings something new. I spend a lot of time looking at food styling, fashion, interior design, and art for inspiration. I am obsessed with social media and check my favorite Instagram accounts daily. I also photograph and share as much as I can, and encourage you to do that, too. I have learned so much by observing my work through a lens and studying the photographs. This is why I'm excited to share this book with you. By sharing our work, we inspire one another to develop new ideas, and together we grow.

Ingrid Carozzi

My Studio

Tin Can Studios is located on the second floor in what used to be a warehouse on Commerce Street in Red Hook, Brooklyn, right between the port and IKEA, and a five-minute bike ride from my apartment. The space is shared by a group of artists, and there are different projects in various stages of development at any given time. Together we form an eclectic community where ideas are often shared. It is a fun and inspiring place to work, and I love this old scrappy building!

The first thing I did in my studio space was build a walk-in refrigerator. The temperature makes a big difference, which is something to consider at home, too: Whenever possible, place your flowers in a cool place overnight. It helps keep them fresh longer.

I built a big worktable for the studio from salvaged wood; I needed it to be both really durable and the perfect height for flower arranging. To store all my vases, bottles, and containers, I had some simple floor-to-ceiling shelves built.

I like to surround myself with pretty things. I never throw away leftover flowers; there is always a little glass or bottle or something to stick them in. It helps with the creative process and makes people feel welcome when they come in for a consultation. But mostly it makes me happy just to look at them!

The best aspect of running my own studio is that every day presents a new and different challenge. No two arrangements are ever alike, nor are two weddings or events. Working with clients and helping them realize their vision is a joy and a privilege, and every day I learn something new.

At Work

Designing flowers for any occasion—such as the events I do for high-end fashion, corporate, and design clients—is exciting and inspiring work, but being part of a wedding—an event where flowers play a central role—is especially rewarding. I like to think that every bouquet or arrangement tells a story, and never is this more evident than at a wedding.

I usually meet with the couple a few months before their wedding day, or as soon as they have settled on a date and a venue. During this meeting, I try to get an idea of the couple and how they envision their wedding day. Are they super romantic or more casual? Do they have memories associated with certain flowers, smells, or colors? Will they be sitting at long tables or mingling around in a park? What will they wear? What budget do they have in mind? After our meeting, I sit down to establish a color palette and a style that will work with their vision and the venue, and, of course, the season during which they will be married.

I am often in charge of décor, including items such as lanterns, linens, and candleholders, but sometimes I am also asked to build larger installations, like a chuppah, trellis, or hanging floral chandeliers. Most of the table arrangements and the bouquets are made the day before the event, and my walk-in refrigerator looks like a botanical garden.

The day of the wedding is usually very busy! It is not unusual to bring a whole team of five to fifteen people. Most of the floral arrangements are made in my studio, but larger arrangements and installations, such as arbors and chuppahs, are created at the venue. Sometimes I stay for the whole wedding to make sure my flowers are taken care of and that nothing is thrown away unnecessarily. (I also make an effort to dress for the occasion, which means I have to work in a cocktail dress and sometimes heels!)

I often suggest we take some of the arrangements apart while the wedding guests are dancing the night away, and transform them into small hand bouquets for the guests to take home as favors. This makes for a sixteen-hour workday, but it's worth it!

A few of my wedding tips:

VASES

- Your vases don't have to be the same. I often assemble a variety of vases, urns, and small cups—some new, some old—and paint them in the same color. I use the same vases over and over.

EXTRA-LARGE FLOWER ARRANGEMENTS

- At weddings, it looks really nice to have a pair of really big flower arrangements flanking the ceremony site or the aisle, as well as on the bars and escort card table. A great way to achieve this without breaking the bank is to focus on branches and greenery and add a few flowers as accents.

CEREMONY DÉCOR, CHUPPAHS, AND ARBORS

- At Jewish weddings, the bride and groom are typically married under a chuppah, meaning "protection" in Hebrew. But no matter your religion, this kind of structure adds a focal point to any wedding venue that doesn't have a natural "altar" to gather around, whether you are inside a reception hall or out in a park. I have made a few different sizes of chuppah-structures, like the one on page 22, using salvaged wood.

- A chuppah can be made in many different ways. Some couples use a swathe of thin, gauzy fabric, others prefer lots of greenery and flowers. When using flowers, always start by tying the greenery to all the posts, then add the flowers. If you plan to use flowers that wilt easily, you will have to use floral tubes (or floral foam).

BOUTONNIERES

- These little lapel accessories are super easy to make! Whether you want to use a big bloom or a few smaller ones, simply pull them together, cut the stems, and twist some floral tape and ribbon around them. Attach them to the lapel with a pin.

FLOWERS AND VASES

Take Care of Your Flowers

Flowers are delicate and need careful attention and respect. If you take the time to treat them right, they will thrive in your arrangements and last longer. Even wilting flowers can perk up with the appropriate care.

First, as soon as you get your flowers home and unwrap them, cut the stems, remove any leaves that would be below the water level, and put the flowers in water immediately. Allow them to drink the water for at least an hour before you arrange them.

Flowers are not all the same. By looking at their stems, you can determine the appropriate water temperature:

- Flowers with soft stems, such as tulips, daffodils, and irises, like cold water.

- Flowers with medium-soft stems, such as carnations, mums, lilies, and peonies, like lukewarm water.

- Flowers with hard or woody stems, such as roses, lilacs, and hydrangeas, like warm water.

- Mixed arrangements do best in lukewarm water.

Second, make sure to add plant food to the water. So don't throw away those little bags of plant food you get when you buy packaged flowers. They provide important nourishment and kill harmful bacteria that make flowers wilt prematurely. If you're buying loose flowers, make sure to buy your own plant food.

Third, make sure the vase that you are using for your arrangement is clean, as bacteria limit the life span of your blooms, and then fill the vase with water and plant food before you start arranging.

Finally, I use a spray bottle to mist all of my arrangements a couple of times a day to hydrate the petals. This makes them look fresher and last longer. I also like to freshen up my flowers before I photograph them. Keep the spray bottle at least 1 foot (30 cm) away from the flowers. You don't want to shower them, just give them a mist!

My Favorite Blooms

1 ORNITHOGALUM

2 SWEET PEA

3 TULIP

4 ROSE

5 RANUNCULUS

6 STOCK

7 PEONY

8 LISIANTHUS

9 DAHLIA

10 ANEMONE

11 CHOCOLATE COSMOS

12 HELLEBORE

About My Favorite Blooms

ORNITHOGALUM

This asparagus relative is not as tasty as its family member but is much more beautiful. Ornithogalums come in many different varieties. I love them and use them when I want to add height or have blooms draping off the sides of an arrangement. Look for them in late spring or early fall.

- Ornithogalums have soft stems. Cut them before putting them in cold water.
- The tiny blooms along the stem tend to open in stages and often outlast the other flowers in the arrangement. Just move them into a new arrangement!

SWEET PEA

According to legend, Francisco Cupani, a Sicilian friar, discovered this pretty little flower in the late 1600s and had its seeds shipped to England, where it quickly became popular. The oldest variety is dark purple and not the pink and white we see most often now. Sweet peas are easy to find in the spring and early summer.

- Sweet peas have tiny brittle stems that snap easily. Cut them and put them in lukewarm water immediately so they don't breathe any air into those tiny stems.
- Use plant food and change the water every day.

TULIP

I love tulips in every color, shape, and form, except when they are all cut to the same height, standing like soldiers in a tight vase. They usually appear in late winter and stay through spring.

- Tulips have super-soft stems. Cut them before putting them in cold water. They also drink like crazy, so check them every day.
- Don't place them next to fruit of any kind. Fruit produces ethylene, a gas that these blooms are very sensitive to.
- Tulips continue to grow after they are cut and placed in a vase and open gradually, resulting in a different-looking arrangement every day.
- On page 60, I show how you can work with tulips and change their form.

ROSE

There are so many beautiful varieties, and roses can be arranged in countless ways. Most roses are imported and available all year round. Juliet roses, tea roses, and garden roses are my favorites. In my eyes the blooms hold all the beauty, so I like to cut them short to hide most of the stems.

- Roses have hard stems. Cut them and place them in warm water immediately.
- They are sensitive to bacteria, so remove all leaves that would otherwise be in the water.
- Before arranging, remove the thorns so they don't harm their neighbors.
- Try not to touch the rose petals when arranging. They bruise easily!
- Make sure to put each rose in water immediately after trimming it; air in the stem will make the rose bend in the vase.
- Your roses will last longer if you keep them cool overnight. An unheated area is best.

RANUNCULUS

With hundreds of pastel-colored petals forming a perfect sphere, the ranunculus is one of the most beautiful flowers on the planet, and I use them all the time. They appear at the market naturally from February to May, though if I ever stray from buying in-season, it is to score some ranunculus! Take proper care of them and they can last up to three weeks, getting more beautiful with each day.

- Ranunculus have medium-soft stems. Cut them before putting them in lukewarm water.
- Remove all leaves that would otherwise be in the water.
- They are not fond of heat or direct sunlight; the cooler the better.
- They drink a lot of water but don't like wet stems! So change the water often, but fill only halfway up.
- Don't store them next to fruit of any kind. Fruit produces ethylene, a gas that these blooms are very sensitive to.

STOCK

Stock is one of the most common types of garden flowers. They come in a variety of colors and can be found almost any time of the year. They are resilient and great when you are looking to add a bit of texture to your arrangement.

- Stock flowers have fairly hard stems. Cut them before putting them in lukewarm water immediately.
- They are easy to take care of. Just pinch the tiny blooms off the stem as they wilt.

PEONY

Originally from Asia, these showy beauties are cultivated everywhere and bloom in late spring or early summer. They are popular both as garden plants and cut flowers. There are countless varieties, some resembling perfectly fried eggs, sunny-side up, others looking more like tutus. Peonies are fantastic as both focal points and fillers.

- Peonies have medium-soft stems. Cut them diagonally before putting them in lukewarm water.
- Change the water every day!
- When in full bloom, they tend to get top-heavy. Keep them cool overnight to delay this process.

LISIANTHUS

This beautiful flower is widely cultivated and relatively easy to find. If you take care of them right, they can last for two weeks.

- Lisianthus have hard stems. Cut them diagonally before putting them in warm water immediately.
- Trim them and change the water every three days or so.
- Keep them away from direct sunlight!

DAHLIA

These stunning flowers are named after the Swedish botanist Anders Dahl, who worked closely with Carl Linnaeus, the man behind the modern system of naming plants and grouping them in families. Dahlias appear in late summer and stay well into the fall. They are great, both as solo players and as accents in large arrangements, since they add such depth and texture. Forgotten for a long time, dahlias are definitely back in style!

- Dahlias have medium-soft stems. Cut them before putting them in lukewarm water.
- Try not to touch the dahlia petals when arranging; they bruise easily!

ANEMONE

It's easy to see that anemones and ranunculus are cousins. They both originated in the Mediterranean area but now are cultivated all over. They usually show up in flower markets in early fall and stay through the winter.

- Anemones have soft stems. Cut them before putting them in cold water.
- Always trim them before arranging or rearranging.
- They are sensitive to bacteria, so remove all leaves that would otherwise be in the water.
- Keep them cool overnight.

CHOCOLATE COSMOS

This fun and versatile little flower originated in the wild in Mexico and is now cultivated in the United States. Its velvety-soft petals smell like chocolate! Look for them in the summer. I use them a lot as accents in my arrangements.

- Chocolate cosmos have medium-soft stems. Cut them before putting them in lukewarm water.
- They are easy to take care of. Just trim them and change the water every three days or so.

HELLEBORE

Hellebore is another cousin of the anemone and was first described by Linnaeus. They are one of the most beautiful flowers I know, and such welcome guests in the dark winter months when the natural selection is limited. They come in different shades of white, green, and pink, and my favorite, deep purple.

- Hellebores are winter blooms with soft stems. Cut them before putting them in water. They like both the room and the water cold.
- They are delicate, so handle them with care and change the water often.

My Favorite Fruits, Berries, and Foliage

FORAGED GREENS are pretty much anything green you can get your hands on and don't have to pay for. I pick a lot of the foliage to use in casual arrangements around my studio in Brooklyn.

POTTED GREENS are another source of foliage that may not readily come to mind. If you have potted plants at home, don't hesitate to cut some leaves and mix them with your flowers. Geraniums grow like crazy and their leaves look great in arrangements.

FERNS are also relatively easy to find and lend an old-fashioned charm to your arrangements.

HERBS, such as mint and sage, mix beautifully with garden roses and ranunculus and look great in most casual arrangements.

VIBURNUM is a woody bush with beautiful white flowers in the spring and red or dark berries in the fall.

ROSE PEPPER is another bush I like a lot. The berries are delicate and the foliage is great.

BITTERSWEET has bright orange berries that make a great accent in fall arrangements.

CRAB APPLES often grow where you least expect them and add a robust look to larger arrangements.

PERSIMMONS are a beautiful fruit that come in the most lovely gold tones and bring personality to arrangements.

SNOWBERRIES, sometimes called ghostberries, are pretty easy to find. They have such a playful shape and add whimsy to winter arrangements.

Flowers aren't only for arrangements. Even a gift
wrapped with simple kraft paper and twine looks special
when accented with a few flowers and some greenery

Bottles, Urns, and Everything Hollow

Almost anything with an opening can be used as a vase: a tin can, an eggcup, a beer bottle, a wooden crate—anything! I love objects with history and patina. Rust and verdigris add such an amazing contrast to freshly cut flowers.

In the studio, we cut and polish wine bottles left over from weddings and use them as vases. We canvas local flea markets and junkyards for containers in materials that seem interesting to us. And we always keep a lookout for places where these kinds of materials are thoughtlessly discarded. For instance, Rockaway Beach in Queens is a treasure chest for scavengers. Way back when, this sand bar was used as a city dump, and you can find the most amazing bottles and containers here. Going on a treasure hunt for vases has become a favorite activity for my daughter, Stella, too. She is quite the expert on old bottles and a budding urban archaeologist. I encourage you to go on your own treasure hunts!

As long as a vase is functional, I can make it pretty, and if an urn is leaking from the bottom, I place a plastic container inside. I try whenever I can to avoid buying the typical florist vases we often see at events. I find them uninspiring to work with and an unnecessary expense. For me, the container is almost as important as the flowers that go in it. Vintage vases have history. They have lived and traveled, and I love to think about those journeys as I fill them with flowers. The instructions for the arrangements in this book list the type of container that was used and its size as a reference, but please know that you can use anything you have on hand. And I hope that you will look around your home, and recycling bin, and start building your own collection of unique vases!

Four Types of Containers

Below are the types of containers that I love to use and that you should keep in mind for making arrangements at home.

RECYCLED: Bottles, jars, and cans, which I have found in recycle bins, landfills, or on the street. I love anything with typography or lettering. It adds character and a sense of where and when.

UPCYCLED: Containers or vases I have fixed up in one way or another.

- For a mercury glass effect, I paint the inside of a glass or vase with Krylon Looking Glass paint, and then seal it with clear varnish.
- For gold-edged bottles, simply define the edges with masking tape, then dip in paint.
- The cut and polished wine bottles require special tools and are a little trickier to do yourself at home. These can be purchased (see Resources, page 155).
- A scratched porcelain vase can be updated with paint.

FLEA MARKET: Used or secondhand items. Most often, I keep the items just as I find them since the natural patina adds a quality that I like. But for some events, I have painted different vessels in the same color, such as brass, to create a unified theme or to add an up-to-date look.

RECLAIMED: Boxes and crates I build from salvaged wood and use for centerpieces. If you are unable to build your own boxes, try your local flea market or garage sale.

TOOLS AND TECHNIQUES

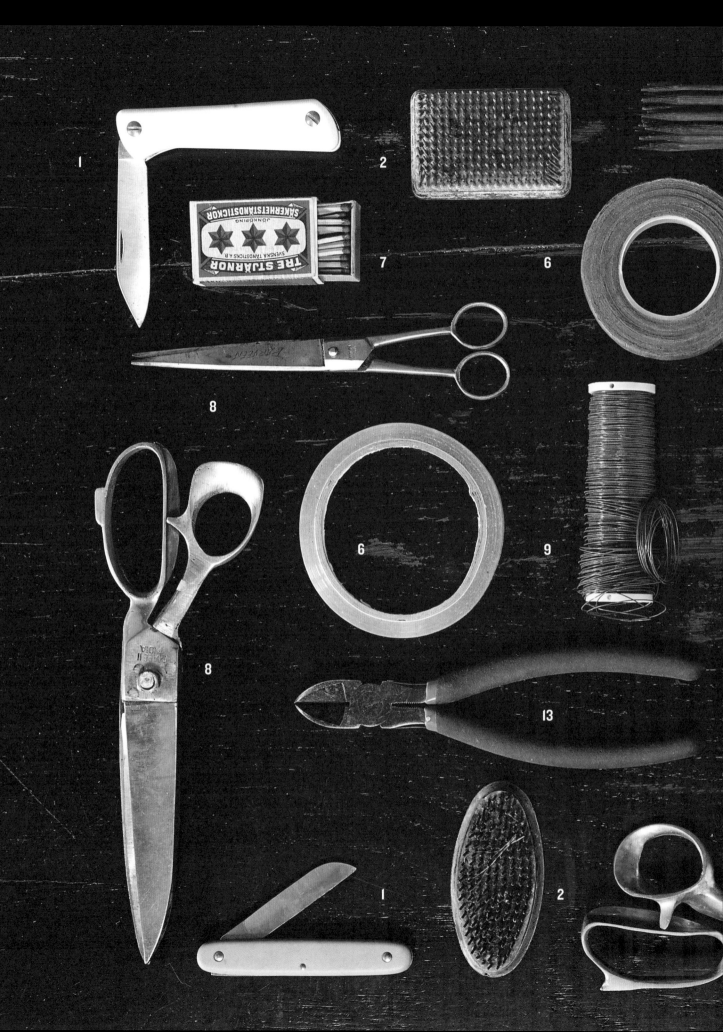

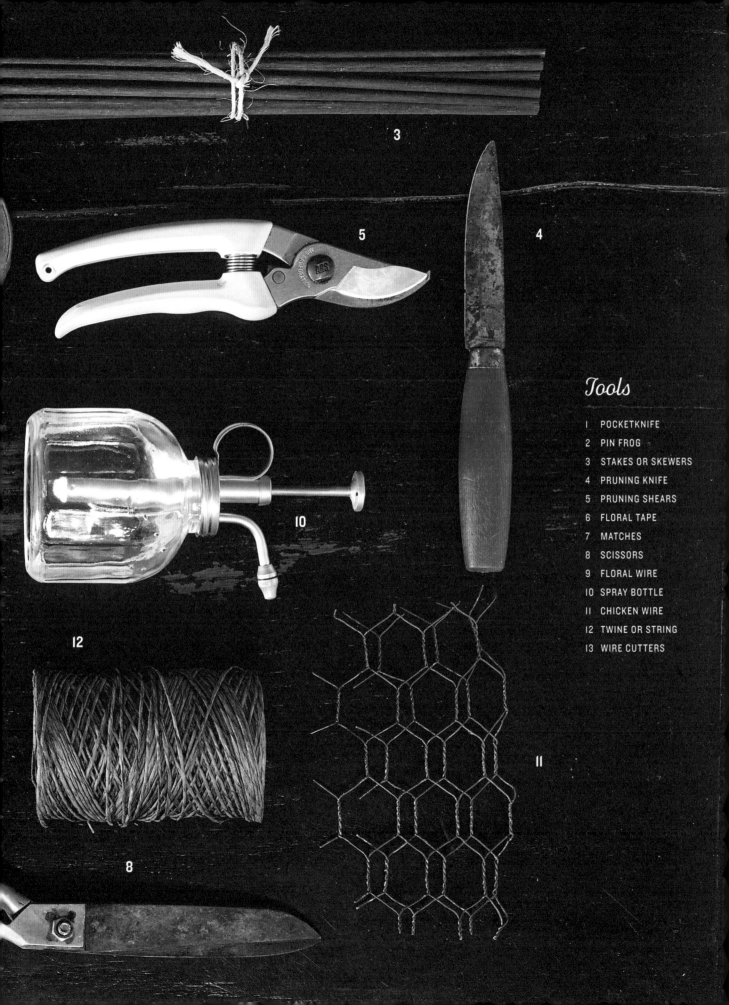

3

5

4

Tools

1   POCKETKNIFE
2   PIN FROG
3   STAKES OR SKEWERS
4   PRUNING KNIFE
5   PRUNING SHEARS
6   FLORAL TAPE
7   MATCHES
8   SCISSORS
9   FLORAL WIRE
10   SPRAY BOTTLE
11   CHICKEN WIRE
12   TWINE OR STRING
13   WIRE CUTTERS

10

12

11

8

Prepping Your Vase

CHICKEN WIRE is one of the most useful materials to have around. The netlike openings are perfectly sized and shaped to keep most stems in place, while still allowing you to move them around. Chicken wire is a must for creating weeping arrangements that spill over the edges of the container. (To illustrate, I have placed the chicken wire in a glass container—though I don't typically use this method when the chicken wire would be visible!)

How to use it: Cut a piece of chicken wire with wire cutters and shape it into a ball. Place in the bottom of the vase. Secure the chicken wire with a piece of floral tape across the opening. For larger vases, fasten the tape like a cross over the opening. Fill the vase with water before you start arranging. And make sure all of your stems are actually in the water after you place them.

FLORAL TAPE is another must-have. When placed over the openings of containers, it keeps the flowers from falling away from one another in the vase. Floral tape is narrow and sticks to wet surfaces well. Use tape when arranging in a glass container or vase, and make sure some of the foliage falls over the edge so the tape doesn't show! Clear tape is preferable.

How to use it: Make a grid by fastening the tape across the opening of the vase—the bigger the mouth, the more strips you will need. The spaces between tape strips should not be much wider than 1 inch (2.5 cm). When done, secure the grid by running a piece of tape around the top edge of the vase's opening. Fill the vase with water before you start arranging.

PIN FROGS are great for arranging tulips, sweet peas, amaryllis, and other flowers with tiny or very soft stems. They also come in handy when you just need to weigh down a vase to prevent it from tipping over.

How to use it: You just place the frog on the inside bottom of the vase. And, of course, fill the vase with water before you start arranging.

Measure, Cut, and Trim

Most arrangements and bouquets are built around the balance between short and long stems—you'd be surprised at how short I cut some of them! When cutting, it is important to keep in mind both the size of the vase and the placement of the flower.

Place the vase at the edge of the table and as close to eye level as possible. (Use a crate or box to elevate it if necessary.) Hold up the flower to the vase at the angle you are planning to place it and cut the stem diagonally where it lines up with the bottom of the vase. Place the flower in the water immediately. Continue to cut the flowers, one by one, always measuring first, until the arrangement is finished. Always measure, cut, trim, and place the flowers *individually* to minimize the time they are out of the water.

In order to see my arrangement from all angles, I place the container on a lazy Susan. See below for tips on trimming based on stem type:

SOFT STEMS are cut diagonally with scissors or a sharp knife. Trim all leaves that would otherwise end up below the water level. Tulips can have thick stems. To make them easier to arrange, simply peel them, as you would peel asparagus.

For TOUGHER STEMS, such as roses, you might need pruning shears or a sharp knife. Always cut them at a 45-degree angle and put them in water immediately!

REALLY HARD STEMS, such as twigs and branches, are also cut at an angle with a set of good pruning shears. To maximize water absorption, crush the ends a little with a hammer or mallet.

For POPPY STEMS, I use matches or a lighter to singe the ends after trimming, which makes them last longer.

Bend and Shape

There are ways to improve the look of the flowers you buy before arranging. For instance, tulips often bend into a graceful arc after a couple of days at home. If you want to obtain that form right away—which I usually do—you can carefully bend them. With a very light hand, just massage the stems between your thumb and fingers.

You can also open tulips to add different textures to an arrangement. Just take the blossom in both hands and softly move the petals away from the center. Hold them in place for a little while and they will stay like that. This is called "frenching." Opening blossoms this way will not shorten their life span.

Ranunculus and their anemone cousins can have bent and crooked stems that are hard to work with. You can reshape them with floral tape and bendable floral wire. Just hold the wire next to the stem and cover both with tape. When covered, you can bend the flower like a pipe cleaner. Since the tape functions like a new skin, it is important that the entire stem is covered. If you want the ranunculus to open a bit more, you can blow softly on the bloom.

The amaryllis has a wide, hollow stem that is made to soak up water and nutrients from the bulb. When you use it as a cut flower, it's best to trim the stem diagonally with a sharp knife. If you want the amaryllis to open faster, make a small incision at the top of the stem and put it in warm water. The opening will let some of the heat evaporate so the flower doesn't wilt.

My Five Rules

I am not a "traditional" florist, and no two arrangements are ever alike. But I have come up with a few rules that I follow.

1. More flowers than vase, please! I often go for a ratio of two-thirds flowers to one-third vase. It is a lush, sumptuous style that reminds me of the Dutch Old Masters!

2. Consider one especially interesting or beautiful flower or piece of foliage to be your focal point. In florist-speak, this is called a gestural flower.

3. Our focal point is usually off-center. Try not to build pyramid- or ball-shaped arrangements; an asymmetrical arrangement is a lot more interesting to behold.

4. Always prime the vase with foliage. Build a base and cover the edges of your vase with greenery.

5. Fill all openings. When you think you are done, step back and check for empty spots. Fill them with whatever you have left over. You usually don't want to see too many stems—unless that happens to be the look you are going for.

Keywords

I don't always use these terms in my instructions, but they are good to know and keep in mind when you arrange flowers.

- *Contrast* is achieved by using a variety of colors, textures, shapes, and sizes.

- The *gestural element* is a flower or piece of foliage that is the focal point of an arrangement. It is allowed to stick both up and out!

- *Texture* is the sum of a bloom's different characteristics and is often used to describe what the flower brings to the arrangement.

- A *blender* is a bloom with two or more colors and is used to soften the transition between distinct colors, to prevent the arrangement from appearing spotted or polka-dotted. If you are using red and white tulips, for example, the arrangement will work better if you add a flower that has both colors.

- *Air* is the space you give each flower. Don't bunch them together and don't let one hide behind another. If there are openings, fill them with foliage to frame the flowers.

- The *special note* is a single flower that adds character to an arrangement without sticking out too much.

MY ESSENTIAL ARRANGEMENTS

*Even though no two arrangements will ever be exactly alike, they usually can
be pulled together following similar steps and techniques. In this book you will see
that I often refer to the following basic designs as a starting place.*

FALL ARRANGEMENT in a BRASS BOWL

Here is a small, very approachable arrangement that can be easily adapted, depending on what flowers you have on hand. Even when you work with smaller arrangements, always measure every stem before you cut it!

SEE PAGE 122 FOR A LARGER PHOTOGRAPH.

INGREDIENTS

1 footed brass bowl, 5 inches (13 cm) high with a 5-inch- (13-cm-) wide opening	5 pink and red ranunculus
	4 large red dahlias
	3 small pink dahlias
Small green twigs, such as huckleberry	4 chocolate cosmos

You will also need: chicken wire, floral tape

1. Shape the chicken wire as shown on page 57, and fasten the tape like a cross over the opening.

2. Arrange some of the twigs around the edge of the bowl. Cut two ranunculus short and place them on one side of the bowl. Cut one ranunculus to about 10 inches (25 cm) and place it on the other side of the bowl.

3. Measure and cut the large dahlias, one by one, short to 4 to 6 inches (10 to 15 cm), and arrange them around the bowl.

4. Fill empty spots with the remaining ranunculus, small dahlias, chocolate cosmos, and green twigs, measuring each one before cutting, turning the vase around as you go.

RANUNCULUS, TULIPS, AND SAGE
in a TIN CAN

This asymmetrical arrangement has a casual style
I come back to often. But however casual you want your
arrangement to be, always measure before you cut!

SEE PAGE 150 FOR A LARGER PHOTOGRAPH.

INGREDIENTS

I tin can, 5 inches (13 cm) high, 4 inches (10 cm) wide

I bunch sage

I bunch long-stemmed thyme

6 to 8 pink ranunculus, different sizes

6 to 8 double tulips

Foraged greens—weeds are fine!

You will also need: floral tape

1. Tape the opening as shown on page 57.

2. Cut the sage and thyme to different lengths and arrange them around the rim, covering the edge.

3. Measure and cut four of the larger ranunculus and place them around the edge.

4. Measure and cut the tulips and place them a bit off the edge of the tin can, working your way toward the center.

5. Measure, cut, and place the rest of the ranunculus, giving each of them plenty of space. Leave one or two longer, sticking up and off-center. Aim for asymmetry; remember, this is a casual arrangement, up and down movement is important for depth.

6. Fill in any openings with greens.

WILD AND ROMANTIC FALL FLOWERS
in a RUSTY URN

When creating a big and wide arrangement, always start around the rim and work your way in, building a base. I often look for a stem or vine that can drape over the edge, creating a romantic style that I love.

SEE PAGE 116 FOR A LARGER PHOTOGRAPH.

INGREDIENTS

1 large footed rusty urn, 8 inches (20 cm) high with a 5-inch- (13-cm-) wide opening

5 to 7 stems foraged greens

2 persimmon or crab apple branches

2 large berry stems, such as bittersweet

4 or 5 dark-red ranunculus

2 large dinner plate dahlias

3 orange lilies

5 chocolate cosmos

You will also need: chicken wire, floral tape

1. Shape the chicken wire as shown on page 57, and fasten the tape like a cross over the opening.

2. Measure, prune, and cut some of the greens, the fruit branches, and the berry stems and arrange them around the perimeter of the urn. This sets the width of your arrangement. Cut and arrange a couple of ranunculus around the edge, too.

3. Trim, cut, and place more greens, working toward the center, leaving one sticking up and off-center.

4. Measure and cut one dahlia so it sticks up over the greens without exposing the stem. Cut the other approximately 2 inches (5 cm) longer. Place both dahlias on one side in the urn. Measure and cut two lilies a little longer and place them on the other side.

5. Measure and cut the chocolate cosmos pretty long so they form spikes when placed off-center. Turn the vase around. Measure and cut the other lily long, so it sticks up, and place it off-center. Arrange the rest of the ranunculus where there is space and fill in the openings with more greens.

MIDSUMMER BLOOMS

This is how I got started as a florist—making
centerpieces in wooden crates for an event in New York
City. The technique is always the same: Start
from the outside and work your way toward the center.
Angle the flowers and think wide, really wide!

SEE PAGE 98 FOR A LARGER PHOTOGRAPH.

INGREDIENTS

I small box or crate, approximately 4 inches (10 cm) high, 8 inches (20 cm) long, and 6 inches (15 cm) deep	2 white or pale green hydrangeas
	2 large stems Queen Anne's lace
Mixed greens	I bunch astrantias
4 white astilbes	3 or 4 delphiniums
	3 pink cosmos

You will also need: chicken wire, floral tape, a plastic box
to line the crate with

1. Shape the chicken wire into a cylinder and place it on the
bottom of the plastic box. Tape it in place. Place the box
in the crate and tape that in place, too. Fill the box only
halfway with water if you plan to move it after arranging.
It is easy to spill the water and stain the wood.

2. Start by arranging some greens around the edges of the
box. Measure and cut the astilbes, hydrangeas, Queen
Anne's lace, and a few astrantias and place them, at a
45-degree angle, on one side of the crate. Measure and cut
the delphiniums and a few astrantias and arrange them,
at a 45-degree angle, on the other side.

3. Working your way around the crate and toward the center,
measure, cut, and place the rest of the astrantias and
greens, making them shorter as you approach the center.

4. Measure and cut the pink cosmos longer and place them
off-center.

SUMMER WREATH

Wreaths have become a staple and I find myself making them all year round: holiday wreaths, crowns for hair, and for wedding décor. This one would look great on my front door! You can use any flowers paired with mixed greens.

SEE PAGES 102 AND 103 FOR LARGER PHOTOGRAPHS.

INGREDIENTS

I wine barrel hoop, I3 inches (33 cm) in diameter

12 lisianthus

3 thistles

15 small *Pieris japonica* stems

25 astrantia stems

Mixed greens

You will also need: clamp, floral wire, wire cutters, floral tubes

1. Secure the hoop band to the work surface with a clamp.

2. Cut all the flower stems short, about 4 inches (10 cm), and tie them with soft floral wire into small bouquets, using three to five stems in each, leaving ends hanging.

3. Start attaching the flowers and greens along the right side of the band, using the floral wire and working your way down and around. Move the band as needed until the wreath is complete, making sure the flowers don't all point in the same direction.

4. Fill the floral tubes with water and attach them using floral wire to the back of the wreath. Carefully thread the flowers through the greenery and guide them into the tubes.

PEONY, ANEMONE, AND RANUNCULUS

Handheld bouquets are arranged using the spiral method, as described below.

INGREDIENTS

I large bloom, such as a peony, to use as a focal point

I smaller bloom, such as an anemone, to use as an accent

8 to IO base flowers, such as ranunculus

3 to 5 delicate or weeping blooms, such as lilacs

Foliage or berry stems

You will also need: string, floral tape, or ribbon, pruning shears

1. Before arranging, trim all leaves and thorns that would otherwise end up in your hand.

2. Start with the focal point, the accent, and a few other blooms, arranging them loosely in your hand.

3. Add the remaining flowers by picking them up one at a time with your dominant hand and crossing the stems over like an X in your other hand, turning the bunch clockwise between your hands as you go, locking the stems in place, and spreading them out like a fan. Don't squeeze them so tightly that you cannot easily adjust them by pulling them in and out of place.

4. Keep adding flowers using this method—cross and twist—until the bouquet is as big as you want it. Stop to check every so often for color and texture. Make sure the flowers are of different lengths. You want a casual arrangement where every flower has its own space.

5. With the bouquet in your non-dominant hand, pick up the floral tape and use your dominant hand to twist tape around the stems—pretty high up since you don't want too much of the stems to show below the blooms when the bouquet is held. Cut the stems to the same length.

6. Tie a ribbon of your choice around the stems to cover up the tape and you are done!

SPRING FLOWERS

—

The arrangements in this chapter feature a selection of seasonal blooms including:

Tulip, Ornithogalum, Ranunculus, Peony, Lilac, Daisy,

Lady's Mantle, Sweet Pea, Grape Hyacinth, Rose

TULIPS, RANUNCULUS, AND HERBS

— *in a Mercury Glass* —

This asymmetrical arrangement is so pretty, and so easy to make. The shape works with almost any flowers, so feel free to substitute and experiment. For additional guidance on how to make this Medium-Size Arrangement Using Floral Tape, see page 69.

INGREDIENTS

I glass jar, 5 1/2 inches (14 cm) high, 3 inches (7.5 cm) wide, the inside coated with Krylon Looking Glass (or similar) paint for a mercury glass effect

I bunch or pot of oregano or other herb

6 white or yellow ranunculus,

6 tulips, white or yellow or both

3 daffodils

3 white peonies

I bunch grape hyacinths

You will also need: floral tape

1. Make a grid by fastening tape across the opening of the jar as shown on page 57.

2. Cut some of the herbs pretty short and arrange them around the jar, covering the rim. Measure and cut one ranunculus twice the height of the jar and place it off-center. That's the height of your arrangement.

3. Measure and cut about half of the tulips, the daffodils, and a couple of ranunculus pretty short and arrange them around the base.

4. Measure and cut the peonies, the rest of the tulips, and the rest of the ranunculus a little longer and arrange them loosely so no stems are visible.

5. Place the grape hyacinths where you can see them and cover any openings with herbs.

TULIPS, PAPERWHITES, AND HERBS

— *in a Vintage Urn* —

This arrangement takes both time and patience. I can't stress enough how important it is to measure each stem before you cut it to obtain the right shape and balance. See page 70 for additional guidance on making this Large and Loose Arrangement.

INGREDIENTS

I large footed vintage urn, 6 inches (15 cm) high with a 6³/₄-inch- (17-cm-) wide opening
I bunch mint or other herb
Mixed greens

4 ornithogalums
12 white tulips
12 yellow tulips
12 paperwhites

You will also need: chicken wire, floral tape

1.   Shape the chicken wire as shown on page 57, and fasten the tape like a cross over the opening.

2.   Cut the herbs and greens to different lengths and arrange them around the edge of the urn. Measure and cut one ornithogalum long and place it off-center to form the focal point of the arrangement. Measure and cut another ornithogalum just long enough to stick up over the rim of the urn and place it off-center.

3.   Now to the tulips: Bend them, one by one, into bows, as I show on page 60. Measure, cut, and place them all around the urn, working your way from the rim toward the center. Fill in with paperwhites and ornithogalums as you go. Fill in the holes with greens.

ROSES, RANUNCULUS, ANEMONES, AND STOCK

— in a Vintage Vase —

This is another one of my Large and Loose Arrangements where you can barely make out the vase underneath. It takes a lot of patience and a bit of practice, but it is so worth it! For more guidance on how to build this style of arrangement, see page 70.

INGREDIENTS

I footed vintage-cut glass vase or urn, 5 inches (13 cm) high with an 8-inch- (20-cm-) wide opening

Mixed greens

I bunch or pot of flowering oregano

4 or 5 pale-purple stock

2 white-and-pink (or just white) anemones

5 large pink garden roses

6 or 7 light-purple tulips

I bunch grape hyacinths

2 red ranunculus

You will also need: chicken wire, floral tape

1. Shape the chicken wire as shown on page 57, and fasten the tape like a cross over the opening.

2. Arrange greens and oregano around the edge of the vase, covering the entire rim, letting them cascade.

3. Measure and cut two stock around 10 inches (25 cm) long and place them off-center.

4. Measure and cut the anemones and one rose and place them, at an angle, on the opposite side, letting them hang way over the rim. Measure and cut a few tulips and stock and arrange them using the same technique.

5. Measure and cut the roses and place them around the arrangement. Measure, cut, and fill in the remaining flowers to form a wide, asymmetrical arrangement. Add greens to any openings.

A MOTHER'S DAY BOUQUET

— *from Stella* —

My daughter, Stella, is my best assistant, and she loves spending time with me in my studio. Usually, I tape and she arranges. This sweet arrangement is made from prepackaged flowers from the supermarket, mixed with flowers from a friend's garden.

INGREDIENTS

I pickle jar, 5 inches (13 cm) high,
  $2^1/_2$ inches (6.5 cm) wide
Lady's mantle, or any light-green
  weed

I bunch tiny daisies
I bunch white sweet peas
I bunch white cosmos

You will also need: floral tape

1. Make a grid by fastening tape across the opening of the jar as shown on page 57.

2. Measure and cut the lady's mantle and tiny daisies and place them asymmetrically around the jar.

3. Measure and cut sweet peas and cosmos a little longer and place them so they stick out a little.

TULIPS AND BERRIES

— *in an Upcycled Wine Bottle* —

I like my tulips loosely arranged at different heights,
and I love pairing them with greens and berries.
The vase here is a wine bottle I cut and polished. If your
tulips seem very straight and rigid, you can bend them
as shown on page 60.

INGREDIENTS

I small cylinder-shaped vase, such as an upcycled wine bottle, 5 inches (13 cm) high, 3 inches (7.5 cm) wide

Foliage (I used lemon leaves)
6 to 8 berry stems
20 to 24 pink and purple tulips

You will also need: floral tape

1. Make a grid by fastening tape across the opening of the vase as shown on page 57.

2. Build a base with some of your foliage. Cut and arrange a few berry stems on one side of the vase, letting them drape over the rim.

3. Measure and cut one tulip twice the height of the vase and place it off-center. Measure and cut a few other tulips almost as long and place them to either side, letting them stick out. Now you have both height and width.

4. Measure, cut, and place the rest of the tulips, one by one, building your arrangement from the outside in toward the center, all around the vase.

5. Fill in any remaining openings with berry stems and greens.

SWEET PEAS

— *in an Antique Eggcup* —

Making this arrangement requires some detailed work, but once it's in place, it will last for quite some time. A Sicilian monk discovered this dark-purple variety of the flower. Maybe it is because of my Italian heritage, but it is my favorite kind of sweet pea!

INGREDIENTS

1 antique eggcup or really tiny vase, 4 inches (10 cm) high, 2¹/₂ inches (6.5 cm) wide

1 bunch sweet peas (around 30 stems)

You will also need: 1 tiny pin frog

1. Place the pin frog in the bottom of the eggcup as shown on page 57.

2. Start with the two longest stems. Place one so that it is reaching for the sky and the other so it's reaching for the floor.

3. Fill in the arrangement by working your way around, measuring, cutting, and placing each flower, starting from the rim and working toward the center.

SPRING BOX

My crates, made from salvaged wood, are my
go-to centerpieces when I am aiming for a rustic look.
On page 71, I offer additional guidance on how to
arrange flowers in a box or crate.

INGREDIENTS

1 small wooden box, about	1 bunch pink sweet peas
4 ¹/₂ inches (11.5 cm) high,	2 ornithogalums
8 inches (20 cm) long,	5 large pink or coral
4 inches (10 cm) deep	garden roses
Foraged leaves and small twigs	2 or 3 white or pink stock

You will also need: chicken wire, floral tape, plastic box

1. Prepare the crate with chicken wire, floral tape,
    and a plastic box as described on page 71.

2. Cut and arrange leaves and twigs around the box,
    covering all the edges. Let some green leaves hang
    far out over the edges on both sides.

3. Start arranging from the outside with sweet
    peas and ornithogalums. Place the flowers at a
    45-degree angle for a wide and weeping look.

4. Measure and cut the roses to different heights,
    then place three a little off-center, facing you.
    Turn the box around, and place the other two a
    little off-center. Measure and cut the stock a little
    longer and place them next to the roses. Fill any
    openings with more twigs and leaves.

    Tip: Only fill with water halfway; it is so easy to spill when
    you move the crate.

ROSES, PEONIES, LISIANTHUS, AND CRAB APPLES

— *in a Canning Jar* —

I love peonies and go all out during their short season, which occurs in late spring. This monochromatic arrangement is one of my favorite ways of showcasing the head-turning beauty of the yellow variety. For the vases, I like to use just about anything I can find in my cupboard.

INGREDIENTS

I large canning or mason jar, 6 inches (15 cm) high, 4 inches (10 cm) wide

2 small crab apple branches

Potted greens or any greens

6 yellow roses

3 or 4 large yellow peonies

10 white lisianthus

2 or 3 ornithogalums

You will also need: floral tape

1. Make a grid by fastening tape across the opening of the jar as shown on page 57.

2. Measure and cut the crab apple branches and greens and arrange them in a thick layer around the rim, hanging over the rim and sticking out quite a bit. Make sure to cover the entire rim.

3. Measure and cut the roses and peonies so they just barely stick up over the green leaves. Leave one peony a little longer and place it off-center.

4. Measure and cut the lisianthus a little longer and arrange them around the jar in such a way you can see each one of them clearly.

5. Measure and cut the ornithogalums so they form a spike on one side.

93

SUMMER FLOWERS

—

The arrangements in this chapter feature a selection of seasonal blooms including:

Peony, Lisianthus, Ranunculus, Rose, Sweet Pea, Ornithogalum,
Stock, Cosmos, Queen Anne's Lace

PEONIES, RANUNCULUS, AND SWEET PEAS

— *in an Upcycled Vase* —

This is an arrangement style that I use a lot. It is easy to throw together and looks great everywhere. It works best when you stick to a few colors, no more than three. For additional guidance on this Medium-Size Arrangement Using Floral Tape, see page 69.

INGREDIENTS

1 cylinder-shaped glass vase,
5 inches (13 cm) high, 5 inches
(13 cm) wide, dipped in gold paint
1 large pink peony

6 pink or white lisianthus
1 bunch pink sweet peas
1 or 2 white stock
8 to 10 yellow ranunculus

You will also need: floral tape

1. Make a grid by fastening tape across the opening of the vase as shown on page 57.

2. Measure and cut the peony and four lisianthus so they just stick up over the rim. Place the peony off-center and arrange the lisianthus around the rim, allowing them to hang over.

3. Measure and cut the sweet peas and place them on one side at an angle. You want them to hang way over the rim.

4. Measure and cut the rest of the lisianthus a little longer and place them on the other side of the vase. Turn the vase around. Cut the stock longer and let it stick up off-center.

5. Measure, cut, and place the ranunculus so they fill in any openings.

MIDSUMMER BLOOMS

Midsummer's Eve is one of the biggest holidays in Sweden. To celebrate light in a part of the world that remains very dark for a good portion of the year, we raise a traditional maypole and pick seven types of wildflowers to put under our pillows for good fortune. In this arrangement, only the weeds are truly wild, but it still captures the natural spirit! For step-by-step instructions on how to make this arrangement, see page 71.

FLOWERS AND BERRIES

— *in a Mercury Glass* —

This pretty little arrangement is made from flowers
I picked up at the corner store. The tiny roses that are
sold in little pots are good to have on hand, as
they can be added to your arrangements when you
need small accent flowers.

INGREDIENTS

I canning jar, 4 inches (IO cm) high, 3 inches (7.5 cm) wide, the inside coated with Krylon Looking Glass (or similar) paint for a mercury glass effect
Any green leaves

7 small pink or peach carnations
8 pink and white ranunculus
I potted peach or pink rose
2 stems of rose pepper (or any other berry)

You will also need: floral tape

1. Make a grid by fastening tape across the opening of the jar as shown on page 57.

2. Measure, cut, and place the leaves, forming a spike to one side of the jar.

3. Measure and cut all the flowers except three in different heights and arrange them around the green leaves. Cut the last three longer and place them off-center.

SUMMER WREATH

Flower wreaths are a big part of the Swedish Midsummer celebration. Historically seen as fertility symbols and worn by young women for good luck, now they appear on children's heads and on men, too, and of course as décor. For step-by-step instructions on how to make this wreath, see page 72.

BROOKLYN HARVEST

— *in an Amber Jar* —

I love picking flowers, and do so whenever I get a chance. For a really casual arrangement like this, you hardly need instructions. Just make sure to cut the flowers, one by one, to different lengths. You can try the recommended blooms below or use any combination of wild or wild-looking flowers.

INGREDIENTS

1 glass jar, $7\frac{1}{2}$ inches (19 cm) high,
  $3\frac{1}{2}$ inches (9 cm) wide

3 stems bee balm (Monarda)

4 ageratums

6 to 8 pink veronica

You will also need: floral tape

1.   Make a grid by fastening tape across the opening of the vase as shown on page 57.

2.   Measure and cut the stems, one by one and to different heights, as on page 58, turning the vase around as you go.

PEONIES, LEMON LEAVES, AND PASSIONFLOWER VINE

— in a Footed Bowl —

Peonies are remarkably beautiful, and when casually paired with lots of green they look less like a wedding bouquet. Here, I have contrasted the peonies with ranunculus, but any smaller blooms would work just as well. For additional guidance on how to make this Large and Loose Arrangement, see page 70.

INGREDIENTS

I low-footed bowl, 5 $^1/_2$ inches (14 cm) high with a 7-inch- (18-cm-) wide opening

Lemon leaves (or other shiny, dark-green foliage)

2 or 3 berry stems, such as viburnum

I passionflower vine

3 large peonies

8 ranunculus

You will also need: chicken wire, floral tape

1. Shape the chicken wire as shown on page 57 and fasten the tape like a cross over the opening.

2. Measure, cut, and place the lemon leaves so they stick out and hang over the sides of the bowl.

3. Measure, cut, and place the berry stems so they hang over one side of the bowl. Measure and cut the passionflower vine even longer. You want it to drape over the bowl, resting on the table.

4. Measure and cut the peonies to different heights, then arrange them around the center of the bowl as you turn it around. Fill in the openings with ranunculus, leaving a few pretty long.

PEONY, ROSES, AND LISANTHUS

— *Hand Bouquet* —

Whether you are making a wedding bouquet or just want to bring some flowers to a dinner party, the technique is the same: stem over stem, cross and twist! Choose flowers in different colors, sizes, and textures, and add foliage or berry stems for a wilder and more organic look. For more information on how to make a bouquet, see page 73.

INGREDIENTS

Mixed greenery	3 purple lisianthus
1 large dark-red peony	5 to 7 astrantias
5 light-purple roses	

You will also need: pruning shears, floral tape, ribbon

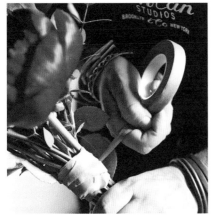

1. Before arranging, trim all leaves and thorns.

2. Start building the bouquet with the greenery and a couple of large flowers with hard stems, like a rose and a peony, arranging them loosely in your non-dominant hand.

3. Add the remaining flowers by picking them up one at a time with your dominant hand and crossing the stems over like an X in your other hand, as described on page 73.

4. Tape and tie the bouquet as described on page 73.

PINK SWEET PEAS AND RANUNCULUS

— in a Flea Market Whiskey Glass —

It doesn't get any sweeter than this! This arrangement is easy;
just make sure to measure each stem so they are all different heights!

INGREDIENTS

I lowball whiskey glass, or small
   vase, 3 inches (7.5 cm) high and
   2$^{1}/_{2}$ inches (6.5 cm) wide

5 to 7 pink ranunculus
I5 to 20 pink sweet pea stems

You will also need: chicken wire, floral tape

1. Shape the chicken wire as shown on page 57 and fasten the tape like a cross over the opening.

2. Measure and cut three ranunculus to different heights and arrange them around the glass.

3. Measure and cut the sweet peas to different lengths and arrange them, building height off-center.

4. Measure and cut the rest of the ranunculus and place them where there is room, turning the glass around as you go.

FALL FLOWERS

—

The arrangements in this chapter feature a selection of seasonal blooms including:

Hydrangea, Dahlia, Rose, Lily, Thistle, Decorative Cabbage,

Chrysanthemum, Berries, Crown Dill

DAHLIA, HYDRANGEA, AND JASMINE

— in a Vintage Bowl —

You'll be surprised when you see just how short some of the flowers in this arrangement are!

INGREDIENTS

1 low-footed vintage bowl, 4¹/₂ inches (11.5 cm) high with an 8-inch- (20-cm-) wide opening
3 large pale dahlias, such as the café au lait variety

5 large white dahlias
3 pale-green hydrangeas
3 jasmine stems
Dark leaves

You will also need: chicken wire, floral tape

1. Shape the chicken wire as shown on page 57 and fasten the tape like a cross over the opening.

2. Start with the dahlias. Measure and cut three of them really short, so that just the blooms will stick up over the rim of the bowl. Arrange them around the edge, at an angle.

3. Cut the hydrangeas and the rest of the dahlias longer and add them toward one side.

4. Add the jasmine stems and fill any openings with leaves.

WILD AND ROMANTIC
FALL FLOWERS

— in a Rusty Urn —

My rule of thumb is that the volume of flowers should be
double the size of the vase or urn, as this arrangement
illustrates. I also really like the contrast between the
fresh and beautiful flowers and the old and rusty urn.
For step-by-step instructions on how to make this Large
and Loose Arrangement, see page 70.

DAHLIAS

— *in Vintage Bottles* —

Dahlias are as wonderful by themselves as they are in arrangements. I love them and can't get enough of them. Here I used five blooms in two different colors, but of course the idea works with any number of flowers. This type of arrangement, which showcases a collection of single blooms, is all about the balance between the colors, textures, and sizes. I played around quite a bit before finding the best look, and tomorrow, I might move them all again!

INGREDIENTS

5 brown bottles in different sizes, any size bottles are fine

5 to 7 dahlias

1. Fill the bottles with water. Cut the flowers to fit into the selected bottles. Each bloom should rest right above the top of the bottle's neck.

2. Move the bottles until you find the perfect arrangement that contrasts the different shapes, sizes, and colors. I like to arrange the bottles so that the colors transition from light to dark.

HYDRANGEA, THISTLES, AND SUCCULENTS

— *in a Brass Vase* —

Since hydrangeas dry beautifully and succulents
are close to indestructible, this arrangement can be
reconstructed over and over. Simply pull out any wilted
flowers and add new blooms or move the hydrangeas
and succulents to a smaller vase.

INGREDIENTS

I tall vase, 6 inches (15 cm) high, 3 1/2 inches (9 cm) wide, painted to achieve a brass effect	I sedum
3 succulents	Ivy or other dark leaves
I large blue hydrangea	5 blue hyacinths
I ornithogalum	3 thistles
	4 or 5 berry twigs, such as viburnum

You will also need: floral tape, 3 skewers

1. Tape the opening as shown on page 57. Cut the
    succulents right beneath the necks. Insert the
    skewer into the bottom of the succulent (this won't
    damage them).

2. Measure and shorten the succulent skewers and
    arrange them on one side. Measure and cut the
    hydrangea taller, and place it on the other side of
    the vase. Measure and cut the ornithogalum to
    about the same height and place it on the succulent
    side, and cut and place the sedum right below the
    hydrangea. Add some ivy to cover the edge.

3. Fill in any openings with hyacinths, thistles, and
    berry twigs as you turn the vase around, making
    sure the arrangement is not totally symmetric.

FALL ARRANGEMENT

— in a Brass Bowl —

Brass vases are so timeless and strong.
I like mixing real brass with painted
containers. For additional guidance on this
Small-Size Arrangement Using Chicken
Wire, see page 68.

RANUNCULUS, HELLEBORE, AND FALL CHRYSANTHEMUMS

— *in a Coffee Can* —

Both the hellebore and chrysanthemums were cut from potted plants, as they can be easier to find in the store this way. For more help on how to build the arrangement, see page 68.

INGREDIENTS

1 tin can, 3¼ inches (8 cm) tall,
   5 inches (13 cm) wide

3 rose hip stems

3 hellebore stems

8 ranunculus

6 chrysanthemums

Herbs

You will also need: chicken wire, floral tape

1. Shape the chicken wire as shown on page 57 and fasten the tape like a cross over the opening.

2. Measure and cut the rose hip and hellebore stems short and arrange them around the rim.

3. Measure and cut the largest ranunculus about twice as tall as the can and place it on one side of the can. Measure and cut the rest of the ranunculus shorter and arrange them evenly.

4. Measure and cut the chrysanthemums fairly short and fill in the openings. Add herbs where needed, all around the can.

FROM FARM TO FORK CRATE

This is the arrangement style that got me started as a florist. For additional guidance on how to build the arrangement, see page 71.

INGREDIENTS

1 medium crate, 6 inches (15 cm) high, 12 inches (30.5 cm) long, 6 inches (15 cm) deep

Garden leaves and twigs

5 berry stems

4 astrantias

6 ornithogalums

3 small decorative cabbages (most of the leaves removed from the stem to form a "rose")

3 to 5 thistles

3 rose hip stems

5 crown dill stems

1 hellebore stem

3 large rosemary stems

You will also need: chicken wire, floral tape, plastic box

1. Prepare the crate with chicken wire, floral tape, and a plastic box as described on page 71.

2. Cut and arrange some garden greens and berry stems around the edges of the crate, working at an angle, leaving everything loose and wild.

3. Measure and cut the astrantias and place them on one side, hanging over the edge. Measure and cut three ornithogalums and arrange them on the other side. Measure and cut the cabbages and place one off-center. Turn the crate around. Place the other two cabbage flowers off-center, and cut and arrange thistles, rose hips, and ornithogalums using the same technique.

4. Measure and cut the dill and hellebore longer and place them off-center. Finish off with some rosemary stems, garden leaves, and more berry stems. Make sure all openings are filled.

Tip: Only fill with water halfway; it is so easy to spill when you move the crate.

DAHLIAS, ROSES, AND CRAB APPLES

— *in a Tin Can* —

I try to avoid making arrangements that mix flowers of distinct colors, as this can create a splotchy, polka-dotted look. When working with only contrasting colors, and no blender flower, I often group them by color.

INGREDIENTS

1 tin can, 5 1/2 inches (14 cm) high, 4 inches (10 cm) wide

2 bushy crab apple twigs

7 small orange dahlias

7 yellow roses

You will also need: floral tape, pruning shears

1. Make a grid by fastening tape across the opening of the can as shown on page 57.

2. Measure and prune the crab apple twigs and remove leaves that would otherwise be underwater. Arrange the twigs around the can, letting some leaves hang over the rim.

3. Measure and cut the dahlias and place them on one side of the can. Measure and cut the roses and place them on the other side, turning the can around as you go.

GARDEN ROSES, HERBS, AND RANUNCULUS

— *in a Tin Can* —

I love when flowers are in full bloom, almost on their last breath. I don't
mind a petal or two falling. Plus, fresh herbs are always an instant refresher!
For more help on how to build the arrangement, see page 68.

INGREDIENTS

I vintage tin can, 5 inches (13 cm)
   high, 5 inches (13 cm) wide
   (this one once held tobacco)
Herbs, garden greens, and weeds

7 small white garden roses
3 larger white roses
4 red or orange ranunculus

You will also need: chicken wire, floral tape

1. Shape the chicken wire as shown on page 57 and fasten the tape like a cross
   over the opening.

2. Arrange herbs, garden greens, and weeds around the whole rim, letting
   some leaves hang over the edge.

3. Measure and cut the small roses pretty short and place them all around.

4. Cut the large roses a little longer and place them near the center.

5. Measure and cut the ranunculus longer and let them stick up off-center.
   Turn the can around and fill in any openings with more herbs and leaves.

WINTER FLOWERS

—

The arrangements in this chapter feature a selection of seasonal blooms including:

*Amaryllis, Hyacinth, Rose, Hellebore, Tulip, Anemone,
Pomegranate, Silver Brunia*

CABBAGES, ANEMONES, AND FLOWERING CARROT GREENS

— in a Vintage Bowl —

Decorative cabbages can really look like
flowers once you remove the leaves from the stems.
I usually remove almost all the green leaves so just
one ring remains around the "flower." This is a
delicate arrangement that requires patience, but
once finished, it lasts a long time!

INGREDIENTS

I short vintage bowl, 4
inches (10 cm) high with
a 6-inch (15-cm) opening,
coated with flat white
aerosol paint

Potted greens or wild leaves

5 light-green or white
nigellas

3 decorative cabbage stems

2 flowering carrot stems

3 white anemones

2 alliums

You will also need: chicken wire, floral tape

1. Shape the chicken wire as shown on page 57 and
    fasten the tape like a cross over the opening.

2. Cut and arrange the greens around the edges of the
    bowl. Measure and cut two nigellas and place them at
    an angle on one side.

3. Measure and cut two of the cabbages really short
    and one a little longer. Place the shorter two near the
    rim, one on each side, and the longer one off-center.
    Add the flowering carrot stems, one on each side,
    and arrange the anemones around the bowl after
    measuring carefully and cutting.

4. Measure and cut the alliums pretty long and arrange
    them to stick up on either side. Turn the vase around
    and fill in any openings with nigellas and more leaves.

AMARYLLIS AND HELLEBORE

— *in Vintage Vases* —

I love to cut amaryllis to different heights,
putting the focus on the blooms. This can be a fun,
unexpected centerpiece during the holidays.

INGREDIENTS

8 vintage vases of
any size

7 amaryllis stems in
various colors

5 hellebore stems

You will also need: pin frogs or sticky putty

1. Fill the vases with water and then start by
    matching the flowers and the vases, deciding
    which stem goes where. You may need a pin frog
    to weigh some of them down, or use sticky putty
    to glue the vases to the surface.

2. When arranging them, go for asymmetry.
    Always put the tallest a little off-center.

ANEMONES, MISTLETOE, AND DUSTY MILLER

— in an Upcycled Vase —

When bringing flowers as a gift, I try to avoid handing over a wet bouquet
to the hostess who has just changed for dinner and is probably too busy to look
for a vase anyway—so I bring the flowers already arranged in a container
instead. This flea market find had an unattractive floral pattern,
which I covered with paint.

INGREDIENTS

I small upcycled porcelain vase,
  6 inches (15 cm) high with a
  2^1/$_2$-inch- (6.5-cm-) wide opening

Dusty miller, or other silver-green foliage

10 to 12 red anemones

I branch mistletoe

1. Fill the vase with water. Cut and arrange the dusty miller around the rim of
    the vase, covering most of the edge.

2. Measure and cut all but one anemone and arrange them pretty evenly. Cut
    the last anemone longer and let it stick up off-center.

3. Add the mistletoe where it can be seen. Turn the vase around and fill in any
    openings with more dusty miller.

TULIPS AND WINTER GREENS

— in a Flea Market Bowl —

Around the holidays, tulips are easy to find. I like
to change things up and cut them different lengths.

INGREDIENTS

1 short bowl or flowerpot,
  5 inches (13 cm) high,
  9 inches (23 cm) wide
Winter greenery, such as
  spruce or cedar

12 white double tulips
6 white tea roses
10 white ranunculus
1 snowberry stem
2 silver brunia stems

You will also need: chicken wire, floral tape, lazy Susan

1. Shape the chicken wire as shown on page 57 and
   fasten the tape like a cross over the opening.

2. Place the bowl on a lazy Susan. Cut and arrange lots
   of greenery around the edges, letting some weep all
   the way to the lazy Susan surface. If the tulips are
   straight, bend them, one by one, as shown on page 60.

3. Continue to cut, bend, and place the tulips, one by
   one, to create a round arrangement, spinning the lazy
   Susan as you go.

4. Add the roses and ranunculus where you can see
   them, leaving one or two longer and off-center.

5. Finish with the snowberry and fill in with silver
   brunia and more greenery.

WINTER FOLIAGE WITH FRESH FLOWERS AND FRUIT

— in a Wreath —

The foliage and pomegranates in this wreath will dry beautifully. But for extra color and life, add some fresh flowers! You can keep them fresh for longer by attaching little tubes filled with water to their stems. For additional guidance on making wreaths, see page 72.

INGREDIENTS

I wine barrel hoop, 13 inches (33 cm) in diameter

I hellebore stem

I ornithogalum

3 small pomegranates

I or 2 bunches soft evergreen, such as cedar or cypress, to cover the band

I bunch dried berry stems (I used tallow)

You will also need: a clamp, 3 skewers, floral wire, 2 floral tubes

1. Secure the hoop to the work surface with a clamp. Cut the hellebore and ornithogalum pretty short, 3 to 4 inches (7.5 to 10 cm) each, and keep them in water. Thread the pomegranates onto the skewers and cut them to around 3 inches (7.5 cm).

2. Cover the hoop with the evergreen, using the method shown on page 72. Try not to make it too even!

3. Cut the berry stems, if needed, and thread them in between the band and the wire, all around the wreath.

4. Now to the fun part: Fill the floral tubes with water and attach them using floral wire to the back of the wreath. Carefully thread the flowers through the greenery and guide them into the tubes. Arrange the pomegranates and attach them with floral wire.

AMARYLLIS, ROSES, AND RANUNCULUS

— *in a Salvaged Crate* —

I love when large flowers are cut really short and hang low over the edge of the counter. In this arrangement, it is so important that every bloom gets a chance to show off, so measure carefully before you cut. But there's no shame in cutting twice! For more guidance on making this arrangement, see page 71.

AMARYLLIS, ROSES, AND RANUNCULUS

. . . continued

INGREDIENTS

1 small crate, 4 inches (10 cm) high,
  8 inches (20 cm) long, 6 inches
  (15 cm) deep

2 ferns

Mixed green leaves

3 dark-red ranunculus or small roses

3 small bittersweet twigs with berries

5 pink amaryllis stems with 2 or 3
  flowers on each

3 large coral garden roses

1 striped or contrasting amaryllis
  stem with 2 or 3 flowers

You will also need: chicken wire, floral tape, plastic box

1. Prepare the crate with chicken wire, floral tape, and a plastic box as described on page 71.

2. Build a green base by arranging ferns and mixed leaves at a 45-degree angle on both sides of the crate, letting some leaves hang over the edges. Think wide. Place the ranunculus on one side of the crate and the berry twigs on the other. Think really wide!

3. Using the technique shown on page 71, build your arrangement from the edges in, all around and toward the center, making sure every bloom has space. Start with the pink amaryllis. Add the garden roses in between. Then place the striped amaryllis slightly off-center. Finish off by filling in any openings with more greenery.

Tip: Only fill with water halfway; it is so easy to spill when you move the crate.

DARK TULIPS AND RANUNCULUS

— in a Tin Can —

Using flowers in a similar hue can be really eye-catching, especially when combined with interesting foliage. You can use dark-red or dark-purple flowers here, as long as they are a close match in color.

INGREDIENTS

1 tin can, 5 inches (13 cm) high, 5 inches (13 cm) wide

Spiky foliage, such as eucalyptus leaves, with long stems (at least twice the height of the container)

1 hellebore

12 dark tulips

8 dark ranunculus

6 white ranunculus

3 thistles

1 berry stem, such as huckleberry or viburnum

You will also need: chicken wire, floral tape

1. Shape the chicken wire as shown on page 57 and fasten the tape like a cross over the opening.

2. Cut and arrange the foliage around the edges, covering some of the rim. Cut a couple of long twigs of the foliage—twice the height of the container—and place them off-center to establish the height. Place the hellebore along one side of the edge, letting it weep over the rim.

3. One by one, measure, cut, and place the tulips to create a round but not perfectly even arrangement as you turn the can around.

4. Measure and cut the ranunculus to different heights and add them, letting a few spike.

5. Cut and place the thistles where there is space and do the same with the berry stem. If you still see openings, add more foliage!

RANUNCULUS, TULIPS, AND SAGE

— *in a Tin Can* —

This is the first arrangement I made for this book,
and it is still a favorite! For step-by-step instructions on this
Medium-Size Arrangement Using Floral Tape, see page 69.

Alternative Flowers

I try not to be too set on a specific selection of blooms when I go to the market. It is more inspiring to see what they have that day and what looks best. In this book, I have listed the flowers I used in the arrangements shown, but you can always substitute. For my favorite blooms, I have a number of alternatives I can turn to for a similar shape, texture, and look.

Anemones:
Clematis
Daffodils
Daisies
Poppies
Ranunculus
  with black center
Tulips (opened,
  as shown on page 60)

Chocolate Cosmos:
Clematis
Scabiosa
Small, dark ranunculus

Dahlias:
Peonies
Roses
Zinnias

Hellebores:
Anemones
Clematis
Daffodils
Pansies

Lisianthus:
Campanulas
Carnations
Nigellas
Oriental lilies
Tulips

Ornithogalums:
Freesia
Mini paperwhites
Spirea
Stephanotis

Peonies:
Dahlias
Double tulips
  (sometimes called
  peony tulips)
Large garden roses
Large ranunculus
  (such as Japanese)
Proteas

Ranunculus:
Anemones
Double tulips
Lisianthus
Tea roses
Zinnias

Roses:
Anemones
Dahlias
Peonies
Ranunculus

Stock:
Astilbes
Delphiniums
  (sometimes called
  larkspur)
Foxtail lilies
Snapdragons

Sweet Peas:
Bleeding hearts
Cherry blossoms
Delphinium belladonna
Foxgloves
Irises
Lisianthus
Snapdragons

Tulips:
Calla lilies
Lisianthus
Ranunculus
Roses

Resources

My Favorite Flower Markets, Nurseries & Wholesalers

CHELSEA GARDENS
444 Van Brunt Street, or 87 Havemeyer Street, both in Brooklyn

I often buy potted plants here, which I use in some of my arrangements. Keeping some potted plants around is a great way to make sure you always have flowers and greenery to cut from.
chelseagardencenter.com

NEW YORK CITY GREENMARKETS
These markets are wonderful since they bring in growers and sellers from many different areas. Union Square Market, on Broadway and East 17th Street, may be the most famous, but there are wonderful markets in every borough. Go to their website for addresses and market days.
grownyc.org

NEW YORK FLOWER DISTRICT
West 28th Street, between Sixth and Seventh Avenues, New York

The markets here are wholesale only, which means that you would have to buy more flowers than you probably need. But sometimes, if you come late in the day and bring cash, vendors will sell a smaller quantity. I usually go to JRose and I always look for Shadow. He is one of my best friends and has taught me everything I know about conditioning flowers. He is also a very, very funny guy. Dutch Flower Line is another favorite. If you go, ask for Chris or Vinnie—they are true experts!
jrosewholesaleflowers.com
dutchflowerline.com

Alternative Retailers to Keep in Mind

CORNER DELIS, FRUIT MARKETS, AND BODEGAS can offer great flowers at very reasonable prices. Once you remove the cellophane and arrange them like I do, they will look pretty!

SUPERMARKETS, such as Trader Joe's, Whole Foods, and Fairway, also have great flowers, both cut and potted, which I buy all the time.

Vintage & Antique Vases

BROOKLYN FLEA
176 Lafayette Avenue and 80 Pearl Street, both in Brooklyn

Open every weekend during the summer, these markets are a must for the collector. In the winter the market moves to Industry City in Sunset Park.
brooklynflea.com

CITY FOUNDRY SHOWROOM
369 Atlantic Avenue, Brooklyn

A pioneer of the Brooklyn design movement, this store is a must for everyone interested in design and the Brooklyn brand! You will find some totally unique pieces here.
cityfoundry.com

FORK + PENCIL
221A Court Street, Brooklyn

This store uses some of their profits to fund art and environmental initiatives in Brooklyn; great stuff on offer, too!
forkandpencil.com

GREENHOUSE & CO.
387 Atlantic Avenue, Brooklyn

This cute store has an eclectic collection of ceramic vases and tableware. I have bought some amazing pedestals here.
greenhouseandcompany.com

HOLLER & SQUALL
119 Atlantic Avenue, Brooklyn
I have found some cool industrial-looking pieces here that I use in my studio.
hollerandsquall.com

HORSEMAN ANTIQUES
351 Atlantic Avenue, Brooklyn
You can find some really special pieces here. Sometimes it pays to spend a little more on an urn or vase that you will love forever.
horsemanantiques.net

SALVATION ARMY
This could be a hit or miss, but sometimes you find a true bargain, and when you do, you help someone else. Go to their website for the thrift store nearest you.
salvationarmyusa.org

STERLING PLACE
363 Atlantic Avenue, 148 7th Avenue, and 352 7th Avenue, all in Brooklyn
Eclectic and unusual objects mixed with reasonably priced pitchers, glasses, and vases.
sterlingplace.com

YESTERDAY'S NEWS
428 Court Street, Brooklyn
With most of its inventory out on the sidewalk, this store feels like a really good yard sale and is one of my favorites.
yesterdaysnews.biz

Online
ETSY
I love Etsy! You can find almost anything here, like the wine barrel hoops I use for my wreaths and cut wine bottle vases, and usually at pretty good prices!
etsy.com

RUFFLED: RECYCLE YOUR WEDDING
Not just for the bride-to-be, this site offers an ever-changing lot of used vases and table décor.
ruffledblog.com/recycle-your-wedding/

New Vases

MICHAELS
Great store to get basic bottles, vases, and containers you can use as they are or transform with paint, which they also sell.
michaels.com

ANTHROPOLOGIE
Their sweet and romantic vases and urns go so well with my flowers!
anthropologie.com

CB2
This is a great place to get simple vases in a modern and clean design. Use them as they are or upcycle them!
cb2.com

THE CONTAINER STORE
They have some really cute jars and bottles here that I have used for events. I also use their plastic containers to line my wooden crates. Super cheap!
containerstore.com

H&M HOME
A large assortment of vases, urns, and pots in a variety of materials and styles at really good prices.
hm.com/us/department/HOME

TERRAIN
They offer a large selection of urns and vases, some reasonable, others pretty expensive.
shopterrain.com

WEST ELM
Nice vases and containers in modern styles, most of them reasonably priced.
westelm.com

Tools & Supplies

FROM THE FRONT COVER

RED AND PINK CARNATIONS, RANUNCULUS, AND DAHLIAS

— in a Footed Flea Market Bowl —

This is a simplified version of my signature style, a special-occasion arrangement I created for this book with your home in mind. It is so lush and romantic, but still pretty easy to make. I used just a few different flowers, and varieties that are easily found, like carnations, an often-overlooked bloom that is so versatile and lasts for weeks.

INGREDIENTS

1 footed bowl (painted black), 5 inches (13 cm) high with a 5-inch- (13-cm-) wide opening
3 to 4 jasmine stems
Mixed foliage greens, like eucalyptus and acacia pearl
3 stems pink spray roses with 3 buds on each, or 9 small roses
9 pink and red ranunculus
4 to 5 red dahlias
3 red and pink carnations
2 to 3 pink snapdragons

You will also need: chicken wire, floral tape, and a lazy Susan

1. Shape the chicken wire as shown on page 57. Fasten the floral tape like a cross over the opening and place the footed bowl on the lazy Susan.

2. Arrange the jasmine and the other mixed foliage around the rim, letting some leaves hang over the edge. Set one jasmine stem aside for later.

3. Measure and cut a few stems of the spray roses and some of the ranunculus pretty short and place them around the edges.

4. Cut a few more roses, ranunculus, and carnations a little longer and place them throughout the center of the bowl, turning the bowl around as you go, filling in openings with foliage.

5. Measure and cut the reserved jasmine stem pretty long and place it off-center following its natural curve.

6. Measure and cut a couple of the ranunculus and the snapdragons longer and place them off-center, close to the jasmine.

Acknowledgments

Thank you, Stella, my daughter, my best buddy, my everything—and the best assistant ever! You are the wisest, strongest, coolest, and most warmhearted kid a mother could ever ask for. I would never be where I am if it weren't for you and your cheers.

Thanks, Mamma Maj, for letting flowers bloom on windowsills and balconies wherever we lived in the world.

Thank you, Renée, for believing in me before I even knew what was possible, and for your continued support. Thank you, Sarah, for being my closest friend and for cheering me on, for always being there for me even though we have been an ocean apart for more than fifteen years.

Big thanks to Eva and Paul, who worked so closely and tirelessly with me through the entire book-writing process—I appreciate everything you brought to the project; and to Ingela, Lisa, and Laura, who let us do our work the way we wanted to.

Thank you, Amelie in London, for bringing this book to Germany, the UK, the USA, and beyond.

Thank you, Shadow, for teaching me pretty much everything I know about flowers, and for making me laugh when mornings otherwise would be stressful and hectic.

Thank you to Chris, Mo, Vinnie, and the entire team at Dutch Flower Line—you guys are the best. Also to Fabian and Dave at G. Page, Smokey and Troy at JRose, and David and Pedro at Rallis—unbelievable that there can be so much inspiration and knowledge within a one-block radius.

Thank you, Grace Bonney at Design*Sponge, for supporting me in the beginning of my career in flowers, along with so many other Brooklyn florists and designers.

Many thanks to Matthew at Recycled Brooklyn for sharing your invaluable creative thoughts and your amazing eye, and for cheering me on.

Thanks also to my talented team at Tin Can Studios: Ashley for keeping things organized; Emelie for always working like a real Viking, never complaining, and still being my friend; Brittney for your support as a fellow florist and businesswoman and for bringing laughter to the studio; and also Emily H., Olivia, Ashley, Chelsea, Chris H., Aviva, Kristen U., Christina, Serena, Anne, Nicky, Jenya, Alicia, Jessica, Nicole, Lori, and Bailey for your support and hard work and for making our world a more beautiful place through the art of flower arranging. Thanks to Kevin for assisting me with install work. Thanks to Liz and Judith for letting Paul, our photographer, crash your wedding!

Thank you *New York* magazine, for naming me Best Florist at such a crucial time of my career. It meant a lot!

Thank you, Chris, for inspiring me through your food.

Thanks to Dannia, Emily, Alex, Sioux, Victoria, Odette, Amy, and Yvette for being my surrogate family and friends, and for always being around and helping out when things are hectic. Without you this would have been impossible.

Thanks also to all my wonderful clients who support my concepts and put their trust in me.

I owe you all.

Kind regards,
Ingrid